Team Spirit

THE SAN ANTONIO SPURS

BY

MARK STEWART

Content Consultant
Matt Zeysing
Historian and Archivist
The Naismith Memorial Basketball Hall of Fame

NORWOOD HOUSE PRESS

CHICAGO, ILLINOIS

Norwood House Press
P.O. Box 316598
Chicago, Illinois 60631

For information regarding Norwood House Press, please visit our website at:
www.norwoodhousepress.com or call 866-565-2900.

All photos courtesy of AP/Wide World Photos, Inc. except the following:
Topps, Inc. (7, 9, 14, 20, 35 & 40); Author's collection (29 & 34).
Special thanks to Topps, Inc.

Editor: Mike Kennedy
Designer: Ron Jaffe
Project Management: Black Book Partners, LLC.

Special thanks to: Amanda Jones and Elizabeth Kjellstrand.

Library of Congress Cataloging-in-Publication Data

Stewart, Mark.
    The San Antonio Spurs / by Mark Stewart ; with Content
Consultant Matt Zeysing.
        p. cm. -- (Team spirit)
    Summary: "Presents the history, accomplishments and key personal-
ities of the San Antonio Spurs basketball team. Includes timelines,
quotes, maps, glossary and websites"--Provided by publisher.
    Includes bibliographical references and index.
    ISBN-13: 978-1-59953-011-6 (library edition : alk. paper)
    ISBN-10: 1-59953-011-2 (library edition : alk. paper) 1. San
Antonio Spurs (Basketball team)--History--Juvenile literature. I.
Zeysing, Matt. II. Title. III. Series.
    GV885.52.S26S84 2006
    796.32'36409764351

                                                                    2005033119

Manufactured in the United States of America.

38888000099758

COVER PHOTO: The San Antonio Spurs hug each other
after a big win on the road in 2005.

Table of Contents

SPORTS WORDS & VOCABULARY WORDS: In this book, you will find many words that are new to you. You may also see familiar words used in new ways. The glossary on page 46 gives the meanings of basketball words, as well as "everyday" words that have special basketball meanings. These words appear in **bold type** throughout the book. The glossary on page 47 gives the meanings of vocabulary words that are not related to basketball. They appear in ***bold italic type*** throughout the book.

BASKETBALL SEASONS: Because each basketball season begins late in one year and ends early in the next, seasons are not named after years. Instead, they are written out as two years separated by a dash, for example 1944–45 or 2005–06.

Meet the Spurs

In basketball, a team can only put five players on the court at the same time. Those players must think as one, move as one, and play as one. That is why many teams try to find players with similar skills, who come from similar backgrounds. The San Antonio Spurs believe that players must only have one thing in common: A deep love of the game.

The Spurs look all over the world for these special people. They have won championships with players from the United States, South America, Europe and the Caribbean. Their locker room sometimes sounds like the **United Nations** of basketball. But once the game starts, they all speak the same language—the language of basketball.

This book tells the story of the Spurs. They were the first **professional** basketball team to play in Texas, and they performed in several parts of the state before finding a place they could finally call home. The Spurs' road to the championship took a few twists and turns—and had many ups and downs—but one thing was always true. When you bought a ticket to a game, you got to see five guys living their dream and loving their game.

Tim Duncan congratulates Tony Parker during a 2004 game, with Manu Ginobili behind them.

Way Back When

Texas is a very big state. There is enough room, and there are enough people, to support many sports teams. Today, Texas is home to one hockey team, two baseball teams, two football teams, and three basketball teams. Way back in 1967, however, the only major sports teams in Texas were the Dallas Cowboys (football) and Houston Astros (baseball).

In 1967, the **American Basketball Association (ABA)** was formed. It was a rival league to the **National Basketball Association (NBA)**. The city of Dallas wanted a team, so a group of 30 *investors* raised enough money to buy an ABA **franchise**. This group included Texas millionaire Bob Folsom, who would later become the mayor of Dallas. The owners agreed to name their team the Dallas Chaparrals.

Manny Leaks of the Chaparrals grabs a rebound against the Carolina Cougars in a 1969 game.

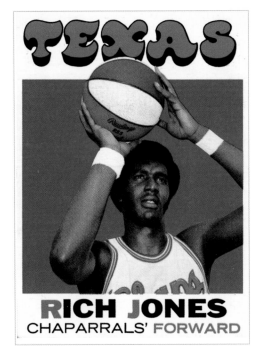

RICH JONES
CHAPARRALS' FORWARD

The Chaparrals were one of the best teams in the early years of the ABA. Their first coach, Cliff Hagan, was also their first star. Hagan had retired after a long career in the NBA. Even though he was hired to coach the Chaparrals, he ended up playing for the team, too. Other stars during the team's early years included Glen Combs, Cincy Powell, Rich Jones, Steve Jones, Ron Boone, Donnie Freeman, and John and Charlie Beasley. After their early success, the Chaparrals found it difficult to compete with the other ABA teams. Hardly anyone went to their games, and it looked as if the team might soon go out of business.

Just before the 1973–74 season, the Chaparrals were sold to a new group of investors. They moved the team south to San Antonio, and renamed them the Spurs. Fans in San Antonio had never had their own professional team—in any sport. The city was best known for its high school football teams. San Antonians fell in love with the Spurs and their **wide-open style** of basketball.

The fans rooted for all the players, but they cheered loudest when their favorite player, George Gervin, wrapped his long fingers around the ball. Gervin was a graceful player who could put the ball in the basket a dozen different ways. He turned the Spurs into one of the highest-scoring teams in history. They won a lot of games, and made a lot of money.

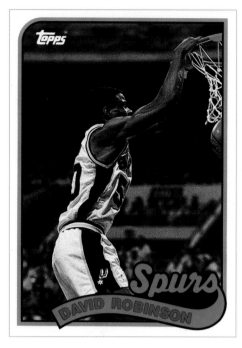

Other teams in the ABA were not as fortunate. In 1976, the league decided it could not continue playing. Fortunately, the Spurs were invited to join the NBA. In their second season, they won the **Central Division** championship and Gervin was the NBA's top scorer.

The Spurs brought their exciting style of basketball to new audiences in the 1970s and 1980s, but they could not win the NBA championship. They needed more than just a couple of great players. They needed good players who could make each other even better. In 1989, David Robinson joined the Spurs. He was a true team player. As San Antonio built around Robinson in the 1990s, the Spurs crept ever closer to their first championship.

LEFT: George Gervin, one of the coolest scorers in basketball history.
TOP: David Robinson jams one during his first season.

The Team Today

San Antonio is famous for a *clash* of cultures that occurred more than 150 years ago. In 1836, the Mexican army defeated a band of Texans fighting for their independence at the Battle of the Alamo. Today, the Spurs are making history by bringing many cultures together.

The team that won the 2005 NBA championship was made up of players from the United States, Belgium, Slovenia, Argentina, and the Virgin Islands. They did not always understand what their teammates were saying, but they *communicated* well on the court. They shared the ball on offense, and worked together to play great defense.

The Spurs have helped to open the eyes of the basketball world. Their success with players from many lands has convinced other teams to search for talent beyond America's borders. And because the Spurs and their fans have welcomed so many foreign players to San Antonio, the city and the team are now known to basketball fans all over the world.

Tim Duncan celebrates with teammates after a playoff win in 2004.

Home Court

The Spurs play in the AT&T Center. It is a lovely arena that fits right in with the history and natural beauty of San Antonio. The park areas surrounding the arena were designed to look like a Texas landscape. Inside the building, bright colors surround fans wherever they go.

This is the third home of the Spurs. They played in the HemisFair Arena from 1973 to 1993, then moved to the Alamodome. Nine years later, the Spurs moved into their current address. It is also the home of the Silver Stars of the Women's National Basketball Association (WNBA) and the San Antonio Stock Show and Rodeo.

AT&T CENTER BY THE NUMBERS

- *There are 18,797 seats in the AT&T Center.*
- *The art collection on view in the arena is worth more than $1 million.*
- *The Spurs played their first game in their new home on November 1, 2002.*

The Spurs go through a workout on their home floor.

Dressed for Success

When the team was called the Chaparrals, their players wore red-white-and-blue uniforms. In the early years, the uniform top spelled out the team's name in script. In their final season, the Chaparrals switched to big **block letters**. When the team moved to San Antonio and became the Spurs, they played their preseason games in red-white-and-blue uniforms, too.

MIKE GALE ▪ GUARD

On opening night in 1973, the fans were amazed to see their players wearing new silver-white-and-black uniforms—with the U in Spurs shaped like the spur on the bottom of a cowboy boot. The Spurs were one of the first teams to use black as an important uniform color. Many people in sports believed that wearing black made players look like "bad guys." Now black and silver are very popular colors. This has made Spurs uniforms and **souvenirs** best-sellers among basketball fans.

Mike Gale models the Spurs' uniform of the 1970s.

UNIFORM BASICS

The basketball uniform is very simple. It consists of a roomy top and baggy shorts.

- The top hangs from the shoulders, with big "scoops" for the arms and neck. This style has not changed much over the years.

- Shorts, however, have changed a lot. They used to be very short, so players could move their legs freely. In the last 20 years, shorts have actually gotten longer and much baggier.

Basketball uniforms look the same as they did long ago...until you look very closely. In the old days, the shorts had belts and buckles. The tops were made of a thick cotton called "jersey," which got very heavy when players sweated. Later, uniforms were made of shiny *satin*. They may have looked great, but they did not "breathe." Players got very hot! Today, most uniforms are made of *synthetic* materials that soak up sweat and keep the body cool.

Tony Parker wears the team's popular black road uniform.

We Won!

When the Spurs joined the NBA in 1976, they were a team on the rise. With George Gervin leading the way, they went on to win their division five times in their first seven seasons. During the 1980s, however, the team had several bad seasons. Luckily, their poor record gave them high picks in the league **draft**. They used these picks on talented young players like Alvin Robertson, Sean Elliott, and David Robinson.

Robinson was an *agile* center who became one of the best players in history. He led the Spurs to the **playoffs** year after year, but they never made it to the **NBA Finals**. San Antonio fans began to worry that their great star would retire without ever playing for a league championship.

George Gervin, the star of the Spurs when they joined the NBA in 1976.

16

The fire burned bright in David Robinson, who joined the Spurs in 1989.

In 1996, the Spurs hired a little-known coach named Gregg Popovich. In 1997, college star Tim Duncan joined the team. Robinson and Duncan looked like they were born to play together. Popovich surrounded them with good team players, and in 1999 the Spurs reached the NBA Finals for the first time. They beat the New York Knicks four games to one, and Duncan was named the **Most Valuable Player (MVP)** of the playoffs.

The Spurs reached the NBA Finals again in 2003. Robinson had decided that this would be his last year.

David Robinson and Tim Duncan celebrate their championship in 1999.

His teammates wanted to give him a "going away" present. The Spurs played the New Jersey Nets in the finals. The Nets did all they could to keep the score low, hoping that good defense would beat San Antonio. The Spurs played even better defense than the Nets, and won the series four games to two. Duncan was named MVP once again.

Now the question was: Could the Spurs win without David Robinson? The answer came two years later, when Duncan led a lineup of *international* stars (including Belgium's Tony Parker and Argentina's Manu Ginobili) to the finals against the Detroit Pistons.

Tim Duncan delights in his third NBA Finals trophy.

The Spurs blew the Pistons off the court in the first two games. Then the Pistons found new ways to stop Duncan, and they won the next two games to tie the series. The Spurs won Game Five in **overtime**, but the Pistons fought back in Game Six to force a seventh and **deciding game**. Both teams played good defense in Game Seven, and for a while it looked like nobody would gain an advantage. Finally, in the second half, Duncan took over and gave the Spurs the lead for good—and their third championship in seven seasons.

Go-To Guys

To be a true star in the NBA, you need more than a great shot. You have to be a "go-to guy"—someone teammates trust to make the winning play when the seconds are ticking away in a big game. San Antonio fans have had a lot to cheer about over the years, including these great stars...

THE PIONEERS

CLIFF HAGAN   6' 4" Forward

• Born: 12/9/1931 • Played for Team: 1967–68 to 1969–70

Cliff Hagan had already played 10 years in the NBA when he was hired to coach the team. When he was needed as a player, he put on a uniform and became a **player-coach**. Hagan was able to use his **hook shot** to score against the ABA's younger, quicker defenders.

JAMES SILAS • G

JAMES SILAS   6' 2" Guard

• Born: 2/11/1949 • Played for Team: 1972–73 to 1980–81

James Silas was the man who ran the team's offense in the 1970s. He was a good passer and shooter, and a great **clutch player**. The fans called him "Captain Late" because he was at his best at the end of a close game.

GEORGE GERVIN

6' 7" Guard

- BORN: 4/27/1952 • PLAYED FOR TEAM: 1974–75 TO 1984–85

George Gervin was so cool on the court that he was nicknamed "Iceman." He **averaged** over 20 points a game 12 years in a row, and over 30 points a game twice. Gervin's favorite move was the finger roll. He would rise to the basket with the ball cupped in one hand, then flick it over the outstretched arms of defenders and right into the basket.

LARRY KENON

6' 9" Forward

- BORN: 12/13/1952
- PLAYED FOR TEAM: 1976–77 TO 1979–80

Larry Kenon had a thin body and a strange shooting style, but he was a great rebounder and scorer for the Spurs. No one was better **finishing** a fast break. Kenon's nickname was "Special K."

BILLY PAULTZ

6' 11" Center

- BORN: 7/30/1948
- PLAYED FOR TEAM: 1976–77 TO 1979–80 AND 1982–83

Billy Paultz could shoot from the outside, swoop into the lane with a hook shot, or use his wide body to get shots close to the hoop. He was big and hard to handle, so fans nicknamed him the "Whopper."

LEFT: James Silas
ABOVE: Larry Kenon

MODERN STARS

DAVID ROBINSON   7' 1" Center

- BORN: 8/6/1965   • PLAYED FOR TEAM: 1989–90 TO 2002–03

The Spurs drafted David Robinson in 1987, then waited for two years while he served his country in the Navy. He was worth the wait. Nicknamed the "Admiral," Robinson won the NBA scoring title in 1994 and the MVP award in 1995.

SEAN ELLIOTT   6' 8" Forward

- BORN: 2/2/1968
- PLAYED FOR TEAM: 1990–91 TO 1993–94 AND 1995–96 TO 2000–01

Sean Elliott was a smooth, confident shooter who liked to make game-winning shots. His most famous was a **3-pointer** to beat the Portland Trailblazers in the 1999 playoffs. San Antonio fans still call it the Memorial Day Miracle.

AVERY JOHNSON   5' 11" Guard

- BORN: 3/25/1965
- PLAYED FOR TEAM: 1990–91 TO 1992–93 AND 1994–95 TO 2000–01

Avery Johnson was a tough, tiny player who always looked for an open teammate. He was the **point guard** on San Antonio's first championship team.

TIM DUNCAN   7' 0" Center

• BORN: 4/25/1976   • FIRST SEASON WITH TEAM: 1997–98

Tim Duncan wanted to be a world champion swimmer when he was growing up. Instead, he became a world championship basketball player. A fierce competitor with a light shooting touch, Duncan was the NBA's MVP in 2002 and 2003.

TONY PARKER   6' 2" Guard

• BORN: 5/17/1982   • FIRST SEASON WITH TEAM: 2001–02

Tony Parker was born in Belgium and grew up in France. The Spurs discovered him when he was 18, and he used his incredible speed to help them win two championships.

MANU GINOBILI   6' 6" Guard

• BORN: 7/28/1977

• FIRST SEASON WITH TEAM: 2002–03

Manu Ginobili was born in Argentina, but San Antonio fans quickly *adopted* him as their own. His *passion* for basketball and his drive to improve every part of his game made him one of the NBA's favorite players.

LEFT: Sean Elliott
RIGHT: Manu Ginobili

On the Sidelines

More than 15 men have coached the team since 1967. On this long list are some of the best leaders in basketball, including Tom Nissalke, Doug Moe, Stan Albeck, and Cotton Fitzsimmons. The team's first coach, Cliff Hagan, had been an **All-Star** in the NBA. He believed that a coach should be very tough on his players. The more Hagan screamed at his players, the more they won.

Another coach who demanded extra effort from his players was Larry Brown. He coached the team from 1988 to 1992. Under Brown, the Spurs learned the teamwork that would later carry them to a championship. The coach who had the most success with the Spurs was Gregg Popovich. He was an assistant coach when Brown was in charge of the team.

Under Popovich, the Spurs developed great team spirit, and their confidence grew each season. He was "Mr. Nice Guy" compared to some of the team's other coaches. But when his players did not work together as a team, he could be as mean as anyone in basketball. Popovich led San Antonio to the NBA championship in 1999, 2003, and 2005. Since 1980, only two other coaches have won more championships.

Gregg Popovich gives instructions to Tony Parker.

One Great Day

When the Spurs won the championship in 1999, it came at the end of a shortened season. A disagreement between the NBA's team owners and players had trimmed the schedule from 82 to 50 games. Many fans around the league did not feel that San Antonio's title was "real," because the Spurs did not have to work as hard for it.

The Spurs worked very hard during the 2002–03 season. No one in the NBA won more games, and no one was playing better team basketball in the playoffs. They beat the Phoenix Suns, Los Angeles Lakers, and Dallas Mavericks to reach the NBA Finals. The Spurs faced the New Jersey Nets for the championship.

After five exhausting games, the Spurs held a three games to two lead. They needed just one more victory, but it would not be easy. The two teams battled hard in Game Six. The Nets led by six points in the fourth quarter. The fans were getting nervous—no matter how hard they tried, their Spurs could not seem to score.

Coach Popovich called a timeout. The players knew it was time to dig down and find something extra—and they did. The Spurs went out and stopped the Nets almost every time they had the ball. On offense, the Spurs made tough baskets when they needed them. When the final buzzer sounded, the Spurs had won 88–77. The victory was special because David Robinson had announced that this season would be his last. "The Admiral" retired a champion, with 13 points and 17 rebounds in his final game.

Legend Has It

Who gave up the longest shot in pro basketball history?

LEGEND HAS IT that it was the Chaparrals. On November 13, 1967, in a game played in Dallas, Jerry Harkness of the Indiana Pacers threw a ball the length of the court with one second left and his team behind 118–116. The ball banked into the basket as the buzzer sounded. The shot was measured at 92 feet and is still the longest basket on record. The Chaparrals marked the spot with an ABA logo, and it remained on the court for as long as the team played in the arena.

Were the Dallas Chaparrals named after a cartoon character?

LEGEND HAS IT that they were. But the character was not the famous Roadrunner, as many believe. It was the cartoon bird on the cocktail napkin of the Chaparral Club in Dallas. When it came time to name the new team, someone looked down at his napkin and suggested they name the team the Chaparrals. A chaparral is a type of bird, similar to a roadrunner.

Swen Nater is still one of the most popular Spurs ever.

Who was the first Spur to have a fan club?

LEGEND HAS IT that the player was Swen Nater. Nater played just one full season for the Spurs, in 1974–75. He was a very nice guy who was friendly with the San Antonio fans. A group calling itself "Nater's Raiders" began showing up at games to cheer for their hero. With his fan club rooting him on, Nater led the league in rebounding that year.

It Really Happened

The Spurs have had two players lead the NBA in scoring. George Gervin did it during the 1977–78 season, and David Robinson did it 16 years later. Each player won the scoring title on the season's final day, and each time it took a furious "shootout" to win.

On the evening of April 9, 1978, the Spurs played the New Orleans Jazz. Gervin had been leading David Thompson of the Denver Nuggets in **scoring average**. But that afternoon, Thompson scored 73 points to take the lead. The Spurs did the math and figured Gervin would need 60 points to pass Thompson for the championship. The "Iceman" was amazing. He scored 53 points in the first half, and 10 more in the second half before taking a seat as the new NBA scoring champ, 27.2 to 27.1.

On April, 24 1994, Robinson was second in the scoring race behind Shaquille O'Neal as the season's final game began. The Spurs were playing the Los Angeles Clippers. Robinson was on fire. He hit shot after shot, and his teammates kept passing him the ball. When the final buzzer sounded, the "Admiral" had 71 points— enough to cruise past Shaq for the scoring title, 29.8 to 29.3.

David Robinson eyes the rim.
He was unstoppable when he got the ball near the basket.

Team Spirit

The fans at Spurs games are noisy and knowledgeable. They know how to have a good time, and they know good basketball when they see it. Crowds of more than 18,000 fill the arena to root for the Spurs.

One of basketball's most famous fan groups roots for the Spurs. They call themselves the Baseline Bums. They have been around since the 1970s, when they were led by "Big George" and "Dancing Harry." The Baseline Bums are hard to miss—they sit right above the tunnel that leads to the locker rooms. They love to **heckle** visiting players, and are fiercely proud of their team and their city.

Larry Brown learned this the hard way. When he was coaching the Denver Nuggets, he joked that the only good thing about San Antonio was the **guacamole**. The next time Brown and the Nuggets played the Spurs, the Baseline Bums waited for him to pass beneath them, and dumped a bowl of the green stuff on his head!

The Spurs have excited San Antonio with their success.

Timeline

The basketball season is played from October through June. That means each season takes place at the end of one year and the beginning of the next. In this timeline, the accomplishments of the Spurs are shown by season.

1967–68
The Dallas Chaparrals are one of the original 11 ABA teams.

1973–74
The team moves to San Antonio and becomes the Spurs.

1976–77
The Spurs join the NBA.

1970–71
The team is renamed the Texas Chaparrals for one season.

1975–76
James Silas leads the ABA in free throws.

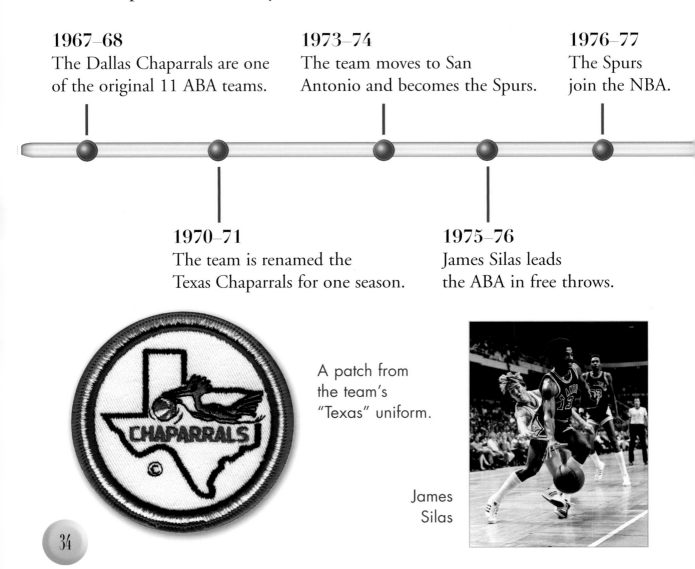

A patch from the team's "Texas" uniform.

James Silas

David
Robinson

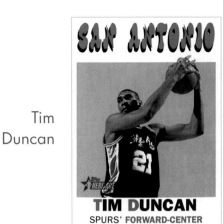

Tim
Duncan

1994–95
David Robinson wins
the MVP award.

2001–02
Tim Duncan wins
the MVP Award.

2004–05
The Spurs win their third
NBA championship.

1981–82
George Gervin wins
his fourth NBA
scoring title.

1998–99
The Spurs win
their first NBA
championship.

2002–03
The Spurs win
their second
NBA championship.

George
Gervin

Fun Facts

NAME GAME

When the team moved to San Antonio in 1973, they were first called the Gunslingers. Their name was changed to the Spurs before the season started.

MAKING THEIR POINTS

In 1982, the Spurs beat the Milwaukee Bucks 171–166. The 337 points scored by the two teams is the second-highest total in history.

CRUISIN' FOR A BRUISIN'

In the 1980s, San Antonio's front line featured some of the roughest players in the NBA, including Artis Gilmore, George Johnson, Dave Corzine, and Mark Olberding. Fans called them the "Bruise Brothers."

Artis Gilmore

Manu Ginobili

GOOD AS GOLD

When the Spurs won the 2005 NBA championship, Manu Ginobili became just the third player in the world to win an Olympic gold medal at the **Summer Olympics** and an NBA title in the same season. The other two were Michael Jordan and Scottie Pippen.

WATCH YOUR HEAD

When David Robinson entered the Naval Academy, he stood 6' 2". When he *graduated*, he was 6' 11". He had hoped to captain a submarine some day, but there were no subs in the Navy he could fit in.

DOUBLE TROUBLE

During the 1993–94 season, David Robinson and Dennis Rodman became the first teammates in NBA history to lead the league in scoring and rebounding. Robinson averaged 29.8 points a game and Rodman averaged 17.3 rebounds.

Talking Hoops

"We had incredible support from the fans we had here...these people were really behind the Spurs. Nobody in the league liked to come here to play."

—George Gervin, on the San Antonio fans

"If you want to make it to the NBA, you have to be tough. You have to have a big heart."

—Tony Parker, on what it takes to be a pro

"Good, better, best. Never let it rest. Until your good is better and your better is best."

—Tim Duncan's favorite saying about improving

"I think any player will tell you that individual accomplishments help your *ego*, but if you don't win, it makes for a very, very long season."

—*David Robinson, on the importance of being a team player*

"I'm so happy, so proud, of being part of this great team. It's difficult to be happier than me."

—*Manu Ginobili, on playing for the Spurs*

LEFT: Tim Duncan
RIGHT: Manu Ginobili

For the Record

The great Spurs teams and players have left their marks on the record books. These are the "best of the best"…

Swen Nater

George Gervin

SPURS AWARD WINNERS

WINNER	AWARD	SEASON
John Beasley	ABA All-Star Game MVP	1968–69
Swen Nater	ABA Rookie of the Year*	1973–74
George Gervin	NBA All-Star Game MVP	1979–80
David Robinson	NBA Rookie of the Year	1989–90
David Robinson	NBA Defensive Player of the Year	1991–92
David Robinson	NBA MVP	1994–95
Tim Duncan	NBA Rookie of the Year	1997–98
Tim Duncan	NBA Finals MVP	1998–99
Tim Duncan	NBA MVP	2001–02
Gregg Popovich	NBA Coach of the Year	2002–03
Tim Duncan	NBA MVP	2002–03
Tim Duncan	NBA Finals MVP	2002–03
Tim Duncan	NBA Finals MVP	2004–05

The award given to the league's best first-year player.

SPURS ACHIEVEMENTS

ACHIEVEMENT	SEASON
Central Division Champions	1977–78
Central Division Champions	1978–79
Midwest Division Champions	1980–81
Midwest Division Champions	1981–82
Midwest Division Champions	1982–83
Midwest Division Champions	1989–90
Midwest Division Champions	1990–91
Midwest Division Champions	1994–95
Midwest Division Champions	1995–96
Midwest Division Champions	1998–99
NBA Champions	1998–99
Midwest Division Champions	2000–01
Midwest Division Champions	2001–02
Midwest Division Champions	2002–03
NBA Champions	2002–03
Midwest Division Champions	2004–05
NBA Champions	2004–05

Tim Duncan

Gregg Popovich

41

Pinpoints

The history of a basketball team is made up of many smaller stories. These stories take place all over the map—not just in the city a team calls "home." Match the push-pins on these maps to the Team Facts and you will begin to see the story of the Spurs unfold!

TEAM FACTS

1 Dallas, Texas—*The team played here from 1967 to 1973.*

2 San Antonio, Texas—*The team has played here since 1973.*

3 Tucson, Arizona—*Sean Elliott was born here.*

4 Tallulah, Louisiana—*James Silas was born here.*

5 Birmingham, Alabama—*Larry Kenon was born here.*

6 Owensboro, Kentucky—*Cliff Hagan was born here.*

7 Manassas, Virginia—*David Robinson was born here.*

8 East Chicago, Indiana—*Gregg Popovich was born here.*

9 Detroit, Michigan—*George Gervin was born here.*

10 St. Croix, U.S. Virgin Islands—*Tim Duncan was born here.*

11 Bruges, Belgium—*Tony Parker was born here.*

12 Bahia Blanca, Argentina—*Manu Ginobili was born here.*

Tony Parker

Play Ball

Basketball is a sport played by two teams of five players. NBA games have four 12-minute quarters—48 minutes in all—and the team that scores the most points when time has run out is the winner. Most baskets count for two points. Players who make shots from beyond the three-point line receive an extra point. Baskets made from the free-throw line count for one point. Free throws are penalty shots awarded to a team, usually after an opponent has committed a foul. A foul is called when one player makes hard contact with another.

Players can move around all they want, but the player with the ball cannot. He must bounce the ball with one hand or the other (but never both) in order to go from one part of the court to another. As long as he keeps "dribbling," he can keep moving.

In the NBA, teams must attempt a shot every 24 seconds, so there is little time to waste. The job of the defense is to make it as difficult as possible to take a good shot—and to grab the ball if the other team shoots and misses.

This may sound simple, but anyone who has played the game knows that basketball can be very complicated. Every player on the court has a job to do. Different players have different strengths and weaknesses. The coach must mix these players in just the right way, and teach them to work together as one.

The more you play and watch basketball, the more "little things" you are likely to notice. The next time you are at a game, look for these plays:

PLAY LIST

ALLEY-OOP—A play where the passer throws the ball just to the side of the rim—so a teammate can catch it and dunk in one motion.

BACK-DOOR PLAY—A play where the passer waits for his teammate to fake the defender away from the basket—then throws him the ball when he cuts back toward the basket.

KICK-OUT—A play where the ball-handler waits for the defense to surround him—then quickly passes to a teammate who is open for an outside shot. The ball is not really kicked in this play; the term comes from the action of pinball machines.

NO-LOOK PASS—A play where the passer fools a defender (with his eyes) into covering one teammate—then suddenly passes to another without looking.

PICK-AND-ROLL—A play where one teammate blocks or "picks off" another's defender with his body—then cuts to the basket for a pass in the confusion.

Glossary

3-POINTER—A shot attempted from behind the 3-point line.

ALL-STAR—A player who is judged to be one of the best during the season.

AMERICAN BASKETBALL ASSOCIATION (ABA)—A basketball league that played for nine seasons, beginning in 1967. Prior to the 1976-77 season, four ABA teams joined the NBA, and the rest went out of business.

AVERAGED—Made an average of.

CENTRAL DIVISION—A group of teams playing in the central part of the United States.

CLUTCH PLAYER—Someone who is at his best under pressure.

DECIDING GAME—The last game of a series that is tied.

DRAFT—The meeting each year at which teams take turns choosing the best college players.

FINISHING—Making the basket at the end of a play.

FRANCHISE—A basketball team, or the right to own a team in a basketball league.

HOOK SHOT—A shot attempted with the body between the defender and the ball, where the arm "hooks" the ball into the basket.

MOST VALUABLE PLAYER (MVP)—An award given each year to the league's best player; also given to the top player in the league finals and All-Star Game.

NATIONAL BASKETBALL ASSOCIATION (NBA)—The professional league that has been operating since the 1946–47 season.

NBA FINALS—The playoff series which decides the championship of the league.

OVERTIME—The five-minute period played to determine the winner of a tie game.

PLAYER-COACH—An individual who performs as both player and coach at the same time.

PLAYOFFS—The games played after the regular season to determine which teams make it to the NBA Finals.

POINT GUARD—The player who runs the team and starts plays on offense.

PROFESSIONAL—A person or team that plays a sport for money. College players are not paid, so they are considered "amateurs."

SCORING AVERAGE—The number of points a player scores divided by the number of games he plays.

SUMMER OLYMPICS—The international sports competition held every four years.

WIDE-OPEN STYLE—Spread out, with a lot of running and shooting.

OTHER WORDS TO KNOW

ADOPTED— Made part of a family.

AGILE—Quick and graceful.

BLOCK LETTERS—Big, squared-off letters.

CLASH—A sharp disagreement.

COMMUNICATED—Exchanged ideas.

EGO—The part of you that only thinks about yourself.

GRADUATED—Received a diploma.

GUACAMOLE—A creamy dip made of avocados.

HECKLE—To bother a performer by yelling rude remarks.

INTERNATIONAL—From all over the world.

INVESTORS—People who risk their money hoping to make a profit.

PASSION—Strong feeling or emotion.

SATIN—A smooth, shiny fabric.

SOUVENIRS—Items kept as a reminder of a place or event.

SYNTHETIC—Made in a laboratory, not in nature.

UNITED NATIONS—An organization that brings different countries together.

Places to Go

ON THE ROAD

AT&T CENTER
One AT&T Center Parkway
San Antonio, Texas   78219
(210) 444-5000

NAISMITH MEMORIAL BASKETBALL HALL OF FAME
1000 West Columbus Avenue
Springfield, MA 01105
(877) 4HOOPLA

ON THE WEB

THE NATIONAL BASKETBALL ASSOCIATION   www.nba.com
  * *to learn more about the league's teams, players, and history*

THE SAN ANTONIO SPURS   www.Spurs.com
  * *to learn more about the San Antonio Spurs*

THE BASKETBALL HALL OF FAME   www.hoophall.com
  * *to learn more about history's greatest players*

ON THE BOOKSHELF

To learn more about the sport of basketball, look for these books at your library or bookstore:
  * Burgan, Michael. *Great Moments in Basketball*. New York, NY.: World Almanac, 2002.
  * Ingram, Scott. *A Basketball All-Star*. Chicago, IL.: Heinemann Library, 2005.
  * Suen, Anastasia. *The Story of Basketball*. New York, NY.: PowerKids Press, 2002.

Index

PAGE NUMBERS IN **BOLD** REFER TO ILLUSTRATIONS.

The Team

MARK STEWART has written more than 20 books on basketball, and over 100 sports books for kids. He grew up in New York City during the 1960s rooting for the Knicks and Nets, and now takes his two daughters, Mariah and Rachel, to watch them play. Mark comes from a family of writers. His grandfather was Sunday Editor of *The New York Times* and his mother was Articles Editor of *The Ladies Home Journal* and *McCall's*. Mark has profiled hundreds of athletes over the last 20 years. He has also written several books about his native New York, and New Jersey, his home today. Mark is a graduate of Duke University, with a degree in history. He lives with his daughters and wife, Sarah, overlooking Sandy Hook, NJ.

MATT ZEYSING is the resident historian at the Basketball Hall of Fame in Springfield, Massachusetts. His research interests include the origins of the game of basketball, the development of professional basketball in the first half of the twentieth century, and the culture and meaning of basketball in American society.